LET'S-READ-AND-FIND-OUT SCIENCE®

# Zipping, Zapping, Zooming BATS

### by Ann Earle • illustrated by Henry Cole

SCHOLASTIC INC.
New York Toronto London Auckland Sydney

*Special thanks to Janet Tyburec at Bat Conservation International for her expert advice.*

It is important to remember not to touch a bat. If you see a bat on the ground, it is probably sick or hurt. Any sick or frightened animal may bite to protect itself.

The illustrations in this book were prepared with acrylic paint and colored pencil on Arches hot press watercolor paper.

ISBN 0-590-18714-7

Text copyright © 1995 by Ann Earle.
Illustrations copyright © 1995 by Henry Cole.
All rights reserved. Published by Scholastic Inc., 555 Broadway, New York, NY 10012, by arrangement with HarperCollins Children's Books, a division of HarperCollins Publishers.

SCHOLASTIC and associated logos are trademarks and/or registered trademarks of Scholastic Inc.

12 11 10 9 8 7 6 5          8 9/9 0 1 2/0

Printed in the U.S.A.          08
First Scholastic printing, October 1997

Zipping, Zapping, Zooming
BATS

When the sun goes down, bats come out to hunt. You have to look quickly to see a bat before it's gone.

Many bats hunt insects. They eat lots of insects. Each night a bat chomps half its own weight in bugs. If you weigh 60 pounds, that's like eating 125 peanut-butter-and-jelly sandwiches every day.

Don't be scared if a bat flies past your head. It won't get into your hair. It's probably catching a juicy mosquito.

Bats are terrific hunters. A little brown bat can catch 150 mosquitoes in 15 minutes. The gray bat can gobble 3000 insects in one night.

Bracken Cave in Texas is home to 20 million Mexican free-tailed bats. Together they munch 250 tons of insects every night.

Bats help get rid of insects that bite people. Bats also zap moths, beetles, and grasshoppers. These insects eat farmers' crops, the food that you and I need.

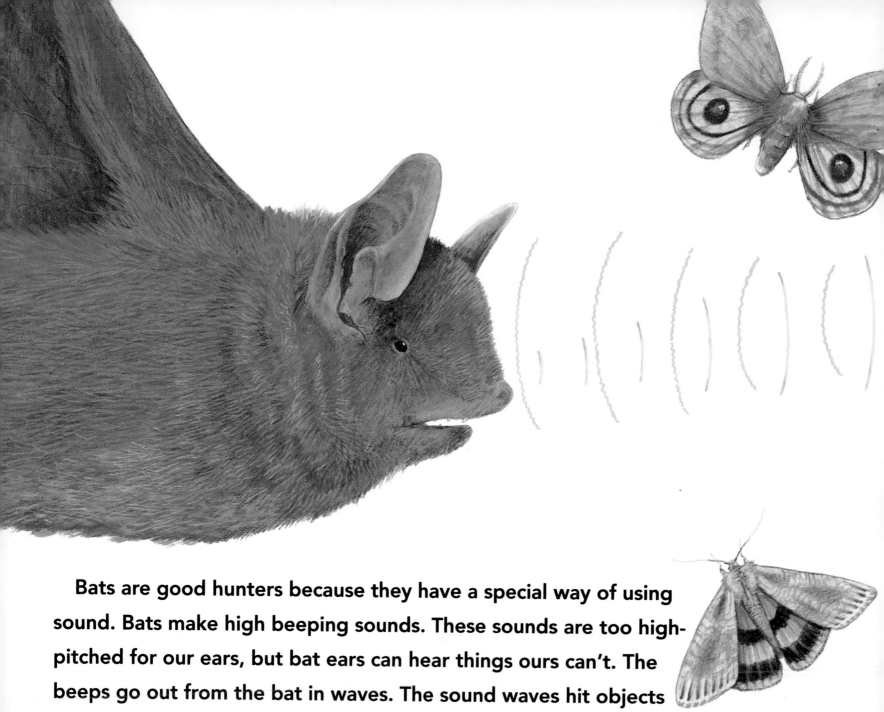

Bats are good hunters because they have a special way of using sound. Bats make high beeping sounds. These sounds are too high-pitched for our ears, but bat ears can hear things ours can't. The beeps go out from the bat in waves. The sound waves hit objects

around the bat. When sound waves hit an object, they bounce back. The bounced sound waves come back to the bat as echoes. The bat can tell by the echoes what kind of insect is near, and exactly where it is. Then the bat can catch it. We call this echolocation.

The echoes that bounce off a tree sound different from the echoes that bounce off a bug. Bats use echolocation to "hear" things that are in their way. They can zoom fast through dark forests and black cave tunnels. If a bat gets into your house, open a door or window. The bat will echolocate, and "hear" the opening it can use to fly out.

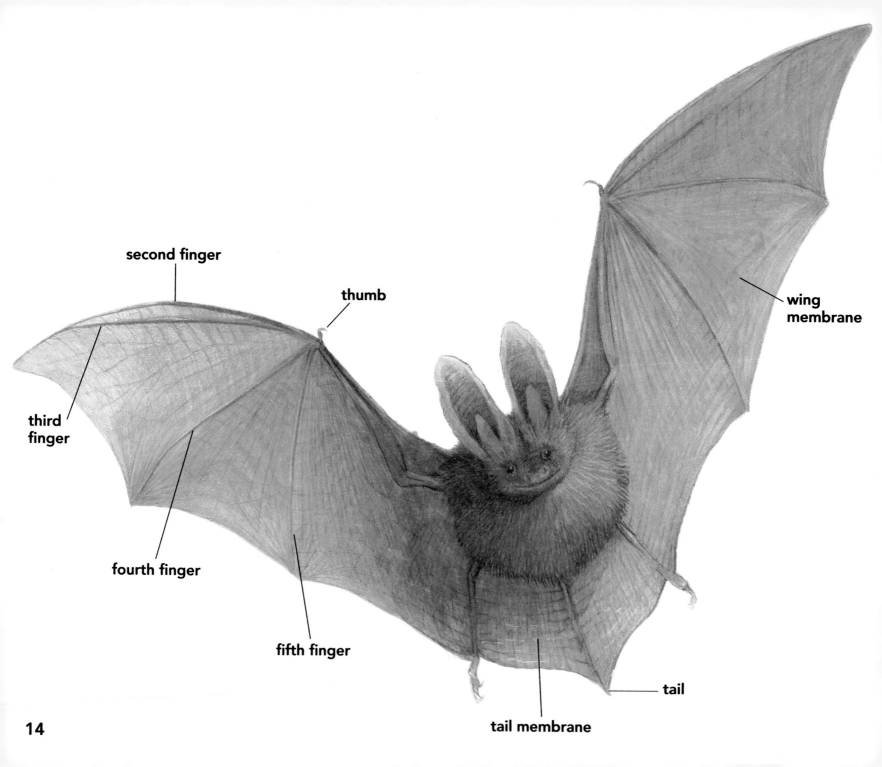

second finger

thumb

wing
membrane

third
finger

fourth finger

fifth finger

tail

tail membrane

Bats are also good hunters because they are expert fliers. Their wings are different from bird wings. Bat wings have long arm bones with extra-long finger bones. A thin skin called a membrane stretches between the bones. The membrane connects the wing bones to the bat's legs and body. It may also join the tail to the legs.

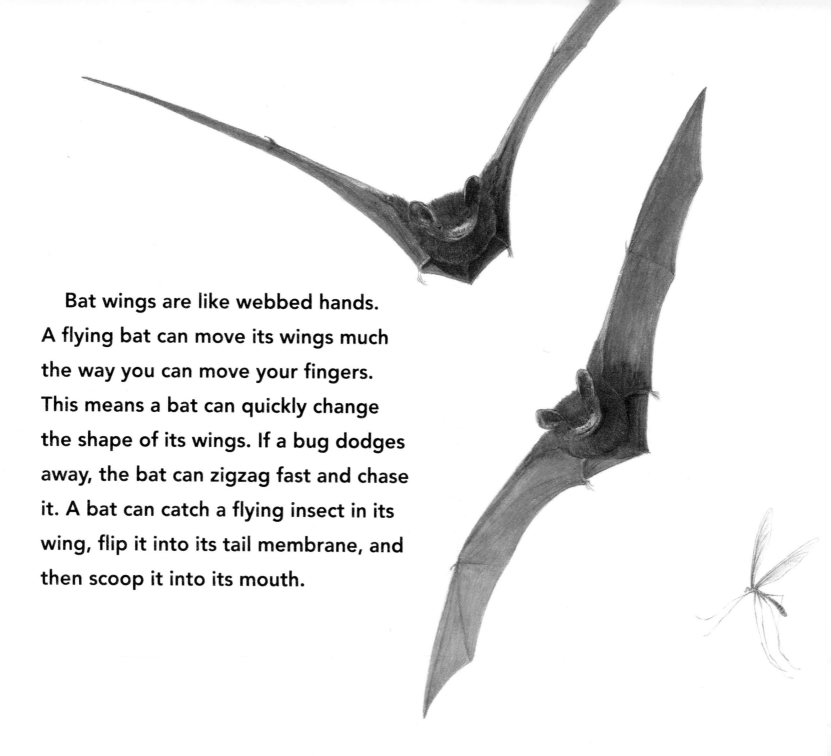

Bat wings are like webbed hands. A flying bat can move its wings much the way you can move your fingers. This means a bat can quickly change the shape of its wings. If a bug dodges away, the bat can zigzag fast and chase it. A bat can catch a flying insect in its wing, flip it into its tail membrane, and then scoop it into its mouth.

Bats have hooked claws on their toes and thumbs. When bats sleep or clean themselves, they hang upside down by their toe claws. They use their claws to move around on their roosts, to comb their fur, and to clean their ears. Bats keep themselves as clean as

Because bats fly at night, many people are scared of them. Sometimes people tell scary stories about vampires that can change into bats. Dracula and other vampires are not real. Bats fly at night because that's when they can find their favorite meals. Bats are really very gentle.

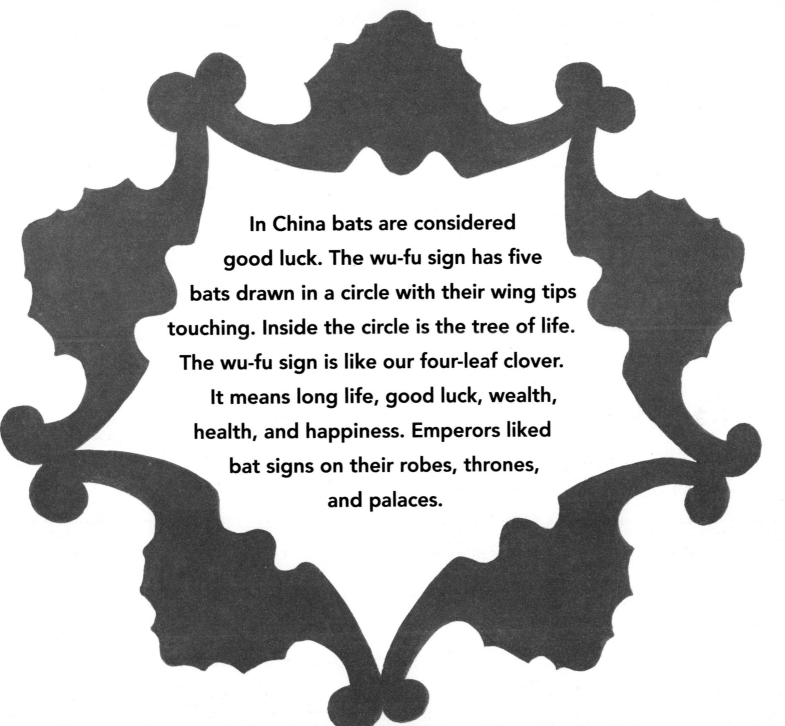

In China bats are considered
good luck. The wu-fu sign has five
bats drawn in a circle with their wing tips
touching. Inside the circle is the tree of life.
The wu-fu sign is like our four-leaf clover.
It means long life, good luck, wealth,
health, and happiness. Emperors liked
bat signs on their robes, thrones,
and palaces.

In winter, many bats hibernate. This means the bats sleep deeply. While bats are hibernating, their breathing slows down and their heart rate drops from 900 to 20 beats a minute. Hibernating bats need less energy to stay alive.

Bats get ready for hibernation by stuffing themselves full of food, especially in the last weeks of warm weather. Their bodies store the extra food as fat. This fat will be their food through the winter.

Sometimes when people explore caves, they kill bats by accident. If you went into a cave where bats were hibernating, you would wake them up. Then they would fly to another part of the cave. Each time that happens, the bats use up about a month's supply of fat. If they use up too much stored food, they will starve before spring, when they can hunt again.

If you go into a cave in June or July, be sure to look for baby bats. If you do see pups, never touch or bother them. Leave quickly and quietly.

Bats are mammals. They are the only flying animals that nurse. This means that the mothers' bodies make milk to feed their babies. Bat pups hang together in large groups called nurseries. Each mother returns to feed her pup at least twice a night. The pups need their mothers' milk to survive. If you disturb a nursery cave, the frightened mothers may leave, and the pups will starve.

Besides disturbing their caves, people harm bats by destroying their homes. People close off their attics and tear down old barns. They seal off empty mines and cut down forests, where bats like to live.

Several kinds of bats are now in danger of dying out. In some places there aren't enough bats left to keep down the number of insect pests. Farmers lose crops, and mosquitoes feast on us. People could use poisons to kill bugs, but poisons can be dangerous to humans, other animals, and plants.

There are many ways people can help bats.

Some people put bat houses in their yards. Public parks and nature centers may have houses for large groups of bats. See page 32 for plans to build your own bat house.

Groups who care about wild animals are putting gates on cave entrances. Bats can zip easily through the gates, but people can't.

In Midfield, Alabama, elementary school children can join the B. A. T. (Bats Are Terrific) Club. Members help spread the word that bats are not scary.

If a bat flies past you in the dark, listen closely. Maybe you can hear the soft fast flutter of its wings before it's gone. Even if you can't, you can be sure that the bat heard you.

## Bat Facts

There are more than 980 different kinds of bats in the world. The bat in this book, called the little brown bat, is the most common bat in the United States. Here are some other kinds of bats:

**CALIFORNIA LEAF-NOSED BATS** live in lowland desert areas of the western U.S. and Mexico. Instead of using echolocation, these bats find bugs by listening for their footsteps or wing beats. Then they pluck the katydid or moth from the ground or a plant. They can even hear a cricket walking!

**HOG-NOSED BATS** of Thailand are the tiniest bats and the world's smallest mammals. About the size of bumblebees, they weigh less than a dime and have a wingspan of just five and a half inches.

**MEXICAN FREE-TAILED BATS** winter in Mexico and return to caves in the southern and western U.S. in spring. The largest colony has 20 million free-tailed bats, in Bracken Cave, near San Antonio, TX. Some colonies have lost huge numbers: Carlsbad Caverns, NM, now has 250,000 bats, down from 8 million; and Eagle Creek Cave, AZ, has only 30,000 bats now, down from 30 million.

**GRAY BATS** are endangered. They can hibernate in only nine caves in the U.S., where the temperature stays the same all winter. In summer, you may be able to see gray bats at Nickajack Cave, near Chattanooga, TN; Rockbridge Memorial State Park, near Columbia, MO; and Blowing Wind Cave, near Scottsboro, AL.

**VAMPIRE BATS** live in parts of Mexico, and Central and South America. They are the only species of bats that eat blood. Most often they feed on the blood of sleeping cattle or other livestock. You can see vampire bats at Seattle's Woodland Zoo.

**FLYING FOXES** are giants in the bat world, with wingspans of up to six feet. They eat fruit, nectar, and pollen. Australia's grey-headed flying fox (shown here) feeds on the fruit of gum, eucalyptus, and fig trees. Without these and other fruit bats to spread seeds and pollen, many tropical and subtropical forests around the world might not survive.

## Bat House Plans

To build a simple bat house, you'll need wood, nails, and some fiberglass screening. Just cut boards to the dimensions shown and nail them together tightly. Some fiberglass screening stretched across the inside back wall will provide toeholds for the bats. Hang your bat house high in a tree or on the side of a building. In warm regions, hang the house where it will be shaded most of the day. In cooler areas, make sure the house gets several hours of sun each day.

For more information on bats and bat houses, more detailed plans, and even prebuilt bat houses, you can write to Bat Conservation International, P. O. Box 162603, Austin, TX 78716.

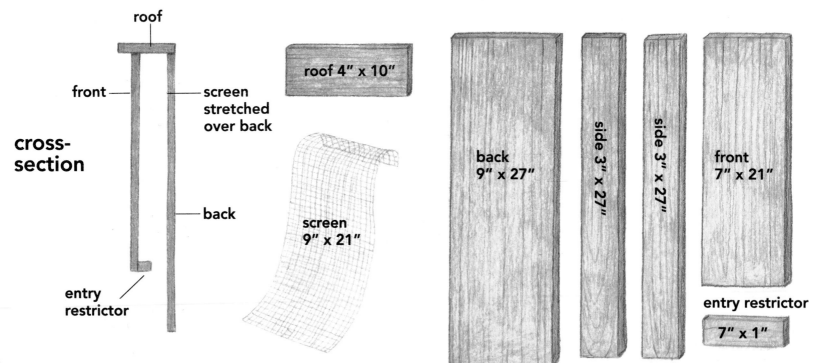

roof

front

screen stretched over back

cross-section

back

entry restrictor

roof 4" x 10"

screen 9" x 21"

back 9" x 27"

side 3" x 27"

side 3" x 27"

front 7" x 21"

entry restrictor

7" x 1"